Seeing Luke
Differently

Reflections on spirituality
& social justice from the third gospel

GRAHAM TURNER

OMG
TXTS

OMG.TXTS
Liverpool, United Kingdom

omg.txts@gmail.com

First published in May 2021 by OMG.TXTS, Liverpool.

Dedicated to all those who see what others do not see
and yet are marginalised by mainstream religious traditions.
Among them are the prophets we need
if we are to inhabit a different future.

Introduction

I was among a number of folk who were brought up with Bibles around the house. We were told we should read our Bibles regularly. Some did this and found the habit helpful and life-giving; others of us found that it was difficult to engage with the text and draw benefit from it on a daily basis. I am in the latter category. I have read some parts of the Bible so many times that the words pass over me because, "I know what happens next."

During the first lockdown of the pandemic of 2020, I was grappling with several changes: I had just retired; we had to remain at home under the government's restrictions; poorly relatives had moved into our home for four months; and our short and medium-term futures were uncertain. (Fortunately, the spring weather was glorious.)

It was probably this unusual mix I was facing and my inner need during a liminal time that led me to look at Luke's gospel in a fresh way. I decided to reflect on each passage from the gospel as a series of conversations with Jesus, written in the form of a reflection. Through these, I tried to express what I thought they were trying to convey, what was unexpected or disturbing in them, and how they might apply today. I wanted to see what I had not noticed before and view the text from a new angle. I wanted to see the gospel differently.

I set myself some criteria: each one had to be between 100 and 200 words and they had to avoid as much religious language as possible. One of my resources was, *The Hospitality of God: A Reading of Luke's Gospel* by Brendan Byrne (Liturgical Press, 2000). In the promotional material the author says, "Luke portrays the life and ministry of Jesus as a divine 'visitation' to the world, seeking hospitality. The One who comes as visitor and guest becomes host and offers a hospitality in which the entire world can become truly human, be at home and know salvation in the depths of their hearts."

There are here just over a hundred reflections each of which will, no doubt, express something of where I was up to personally in the disruptive year of 2020. They are not an exhaustive consideration of each passage, but I hope are still adequate to be an aid for journeying with the gospel again or even if looking at this part of the Bible for the first time. It will probably be helpful to look at the relevant verses from Luke before reading each of them, but this is not always necessary as many of them have a message to communicate even when read alone.

While it is useful to consider how much common ground you find with what I have written, it is also important to take the enquiry a bit further. How do these reflections impinge on who you think you are as a person, and what you feel about the part you play on the stage of life? And then, in what ways is life calling you, not just to pray and reflect differently, but live differently in a complex, wonderful and worrying world?

Contents

Prayer and the future of our species

Luke 1.1-4

Good news God, we thank you for Dr. Luke,
    a man careful, precise and passionate in being a faithful witness
    of what he saw and what he experienced.
We covet a name like "Theophilus";[1]
    we also would like to be known as lovers of God.
In the reading of this gospel
    help us take our place in the Great Tradition[2]
    of all those who have gone before us,
    especially those others who also set down orderly accounts
    of these world-changing events.
We want to know the truth, not as dry objective information,
    but by participation in your life.
We want to know this truth as we too want to be free.
Amen.

---

[1] The Greek name *Theophilus* means "lover of God".
[2] This is the tradition that stretches back to before Jesus, through the Old
Testament to the Sinai covenant and further still to Abraham.

Luke 1.5-25

In the shadow of an ugly tyrant King,
    Zechariah and Elizabeth practised their faith
    living according to the spirit of the law as well as its letter.
They carried a sadness and suffered a disgrace though,
    for they were old and childless.
In the majesty of the temple
    Zechariah, a priest, was called upon
    to perform the greatest of honours,
    to enter into the most special place, alone.
But Lord, he suffered a terrible shock
    meeting you there in your angel.
He was told, "Do not fear,
    you will have joy and gladness,
    Elizabeth will have a baby and you must call him John.
This child will be great,
    great in the sight of God rather than people:
    he will be God-filled;
    he will lead many to Israel's God;
    he will carry the mark of Elijah;
    he will make ready a people for the Lord."
Unbelievable! So thought Zechariah.
Consequently, he was not able or allowed to speak
    until the child was born, ironically,
    as the child would have so much to so many.
Lord, remove the disgrace of many who suffer shame today,
    that they too may live God-filled lives.
Amen.

Luke 1.26-38

We do not easily believe we are also favoured
    or that you are present to us.
Teach us not to fear being perplexed
    or questioning what your purposes are for us.
You sometimes ask of us things apparently ridiculous and bizarre;
    at other times you ask us to continue
    faithfully in the ordinary and mundane rhythms of life.
Anything you ask of us will be great in your economy,
    even though we sadly grade and compare our various callings.
Let us learn from Mary
    and be open, available and non-judgemental,
    saying, "Let it be to me,"
    as we also may have no idea where your leading
    will eventually take us.
We believe so many things to be impossible,
    however, nothing will be impossible with you.
Amen.

Luke 1.39-56

My true self enlarges your life in and around me,
    the core of my being is joyful in you, O Great Love,
    for you have looked out for the little people of life.
Many will see and know something has happened
    because of your love bearing down.
Mercy is your default setting for all who seek you out.
You are strong in humility
    which circumvents the tactics of devious schemers.
Many of the elite have found themselves falling
    when their preconceived ideas
    and assumptions ran out of steam.
But there are multiple stories
    of those you have lifted up out of the ditch
    and countless people who have known
    your unexpected provision.
Those who believe they are self-made because of their wealth
    will finally remain on the side-lines feeling empty.
You have always been a God who helps
    (in the best sense of the word)
    and you have remembered your commitment to all humanity.
Thank you.
Amen.

Luke 1.57-66

O Infinite Life, you expect much of some folk,
    in this instance he was called John, *Yohanan,*[3]
    "The Lord is hospitable and courteous."
Sometimes you silence us in our disbelief, for
    we do not believe you still act today,
    we do not believe you can break open our collective deadness
    and, to be honest, we do not still believe *in* you;
    we generally function as atheists.
But there are those amongst us
    who have not lost that great longing or connection,
    often the marginalised who doggedly hang on to your goodness
    and are still able to rejoice and sing and dance.
Raise up those who will not hold back on what they'll say
    nor be consumed with protecting their reputations.
Raise up those who can see clearly the evil that destroys all life.
Raise up those who have nothing to lose
    as they know they already possess all things.
Give us some more "Johns"
    (on whom we can see the hand of God)
    to turn our worlds upside down.
Amen.

---

[3] *Yohanan* is a transliteration into the Latin alphabet of the Hebrew name John (here talking of John the Baptist).

Luke 1.67-80

O congratulated[1] and contented God,
    you look with positive regard to regain your people.
You have raised up a liberator from among us.
Just as you have repeated over the aeons of history,
    you will act again;
    you are consistent with your promises of old,
    for you are a congruent God.
You have promised:
    we will not forever face enemies and opposition;
    we will not live endlessly in a culture of decline; and
    we will not always live on a planet of destruction.
So we will work and serve without terror or anxiety
    for the good of all people and creation,
    for as long as our strength permits.
Baptiser John will always be known
    as the prophet of the Most High
    for, until him, no word had been heard from you
    in four hundred years.
But now dawn has tenderly come following a long period of night
    and those entrapped in the shadow of death
    have found a guiding light.
Give us such children again in whom, during their earliest months
    and years, we can see the mark of the Most High.
Amen.

---

[1] The Greek word *makarioi* (Luke 1.68) is usually translated as "Blessed". Unfortunately this tends to give the word an overly religious feel. "Happy" can seem rather trite. Christopher Jamison, in his book *Finding Happiness* uses the word congratulations in place of blessed when the word occurs in the Beatitudes.

Luke 2.1-20

Talk of emperors and powerful men publishing decrees
    makes us feel uncertain and concerned,
    these are usually not for our good.
We live in a digital environment that constantly
    measures and records our activity,
    counting and tallying what we do each day.
There are many like Mary today
    who are pawns in the political and commercial systems of life.
There are many who are at delicate stages of life,
    where the dark unknown haunts them
    as they make their way precariously through each day.
Yet, it was into such darkness
    you sent your gift of life and love.
It was into the hands of the strong parental love
    of Mary and Joseph that precariousness was born.
In the middle of such a tentative and fragile situation
    you called men to see Jesus.
These were not powerful men of decrees and degrees,
    these were shepherd men, considered low-life,
    even though high and religious men required their sheep
    to indulge elite piety.
May we be humble and joyful as they were humble and joyful.
May we ponder and treasure the most important things of life,
    as Mary did.
Amen.

Luke 2.15-21

The plan started as you continued it thirty years later,
    mixing with those considered contemptible
    and disreputable.
Marginal men from marginal lands were
    the first to be told,
    the first to see
    and the first to be amazed.
In visiting your stable-bound presence,
    sheep-men jumped the queue to see the monarch-in-waiting.
The pattern is true in your economy
    even before you pronounce,
    "The first shall be last and the last shall be first."
Like Mary, they were among the early evangelists,
    making known what they knew and had been told.
Teach us to honour what the world despises
    and learn from those it excludes,
    for it is to oddballs, misfits, sinners, unhygienics,
    foreigners, children and dodgy types
    that the great secret is given.
The saying is true,
    "Only those who do not need power can be trusted with it."
Thanks be to God.
Amen.

Luke 2.21-40

Again, humility shadowed you even in your early years,
    a couple of pigeons and an ageing man
    became the audience that day.
"Governor," wise old Simeon said,
    "My time is up, your work is done,
    the urge and direction of history
    have been completed right before my eyes in this community.
Outsiders and insiders together will see.
Outsiders and insiders together will journey to wholeness.
Outsiders and insiders together will be your people."
Lord, we are uncomfortable with you being
    destined for the falling of many,
    as a sign to be opposed,
    or the one who will expose inner thoughts.
This does not sit easily with our vested interests.
We are also amazed and alarmed that you call people to suffering
    where souls will be pierced with pain
    and many hopes dashed.
Amid such threat and peril
    make us a people who can still live in delight of you.
Amen.

Luke 2.41-52

O festival God,[5] we look down on children
    describing them as the church of tomorrow,
    those who still have much to learn from us.
We even despise their childish ways
    preferring them to fit into our grown-up ways of being religious
    rather than allowing the child to lead us.
Help us to see as they see.
Help us to be born again.
Help us to find again the innocence we have lost
    through wounding and pain.
Help us to recognise that knowing things is not wisdom
    and age does not give us an advantage
    unless we tread the downward path of growth.
Help us not to idolise our children
    but give them what is essential for their nurture.
Once more, may we treasure what we see each day
    so we see you in all things.
Amen.

---

[5] This was the annual festival of Passover.

Luke 3.1-6

O Word of God, Eternal Christ,
    you came to John
    during the people's long years of foreign occupation,
    religious oppression and utter hopelessness.
While top pietistic leaders were divided one against the other,
    your people suffered under a monarch,
    a governor and an emperor.
O Word of God, Eternal Christ,
    you came to John during his long days in wild
    and forgotten places,
    while he looked and longed and hoped.
Take us back to your life-levelling,
    straightened pathways, in which every expression of life
    will see your cosmic-wide healing.
Take us back,
    so we surrender our long-held commitment
    to mind-boggling, complex theories of how you work.
Relieve us from our crooked, tortuous paths
    with their wilful up-and-down ways.
Amen.

Luke 3.7-14

While in our malice and ill-will,
    you call us, via the prophet John, bastard snakes[6]
    who flee as from forest infernos.
While in our fearful, established attitudes
    we only see fire as life-destroying and reducing.
While in our desperation
    we cling onto our lifeless heritages
    and our long-held sense of spiritual entitlement
    in the vain hope they will offer us a reprieve.
But for you Lord, fire is the energy of life that brings newness
    by cremating our deadness and fake veneers.
You call us to demonstrate our baptism now by
    practising economic justice, living in true honesty,
    and being contented people.
So come with your baptism of life-giving fire
    and your pruning knife
    to remove all that has already died in us.
First though, give us courage
    that we may see beyond all that threatens
    our power, prestige and self-image,
    to recognise the resurrection fruit that will surely then emerge.
Amen.

---

[6] The phrase "offspring (or generation) of vipers" (Luke 3.7) implies children not from a legitimate union. Thus "bastard snakes" can be considered a better translation in that context. This, of course, needs reinterpreting for today.

Luke 3.15-22

O God, we too hear the shouted words of Prophet John
    over and across the clamour of people
    who are full of questions and expectations
    and yearn for a better life than the little they have inherited.
We too hear the quiet words of John
    who simply states his lack of worthiness
    to hold and unlace the master's shoe.
But fire and love are coming in an inundating baptism
    which will upset rulers and leaders,
    all those with much to lose.
Today we pray for those who, like John,
    sit in locked and guarded cells,
    imprisoned with their thoughts and lack of liberty.
We note the voice from heaven
    toward the much beloved Son
    who is enveloped in the embrace of heavenly acceptance.
All we can do is stand and watch
    and sense, with open awareness.
The Love-God is here.
Amen.

Luke 3.23-38

Son of Adam, Son of God,
    you were deeply embedded in our tradition
    and rooted in our humanity.
Among your ancestors
    you counted those known and unknown,
    many with a dubious track record
    and many who lived faithfully within your promise.
Son of Adam, Son of God,
    you are not alien to us
    and neither are we strangers to you,
    for in flesh and blood you lived the gift of life
    and in love and suffering you increased.
May we not despise those who have gone before us
    nor forget our solidarity with them,
    for we are not greater than they;
    we all share the same molecules and atoms,
    hopes and fears.
Son of Adam, Son of God, hear our prayer today.
Amen.

Luke 4.1-13

O Son of God,
 the hunger of austerity took you to private and personal places
 we do not dare to enter.
In the bleak wildness of empty spaces
 you battled against taking the easy route through life;
 you rejected the seductions of cheap surrender,
 power and spectacle.
The devil was in the detail and corruption in the subtleties
 of arguments put so simply and smoothly.
The erosion of our confidence
 in the life you have placed within us
 takes effect too quickly
 leading us
 to trust what is "outer" rather than all that is "inner".
O Son of God,
 you did not complete your ordeal beaten down and exhausted,
 but full of Spirit and sure of the affirmation of the voice
 from beyond and behind our reality.
Give us a confidence in our calling
 to also be called daughters and sons of God.
Amen.

Luke 4.14-21

O power-filled Jesus,
    we have not forgotten the day you went public
    in your home town.
Your urge was not to lord it over others,
    nor to enjoy privilege or prestige,
    nor to dictate and dominate.
In reading the scripts of Isaiah, the prophet of old,
    you humbled yourself to the tradition of texts
    and their spirituality.
You took your place within the cloud of witnesses
    who had spoken so faithfully and often out of season,
    thus paying the ultimate price.
They spoke and you spoke with great compassion
    for those who are poor,
    for those who are prisoners,
    for those who are blind,
    for those who are oppressed
    and for all who seek jubilee freedom.
It is not often we hear such humble power.
Make us stand up to speak out and to act decisively
    for the sake of those who hang out
    in dark and difficult places.
Amen.

Luke 4.21-30

O Son of Joseph,
    you made your mark at the weekly service;
    all were impressed by how you spoke,
    especially being a home-grown local boy.
But you were not impressed by their need to control you
    and hold you close to their community,
    to own you as their worship leader and preacher.
You are not only son of Joseph, you are Son of God.
To our fearful hearts, you seem needlessly provocative
    and greatly impolite to those who highly laud you.
But you will not be corralled or contained by others' small agendas
    or sycophantic hearts.
You will not provide a drama for them
    as a re-enactment of love placed elsewhere.
You are a prophet in the same vein as Elijah and Elisha
    who exercised their energies
    for the sake of outsiders and foreigners.
O son of Joseph,
    you made your mark when you rejected
    your hometown's call to remain and be their local hero.
O Son of God,
    you walked so close to death
    and almost lost it all at the start.
But nothing will stop your direction and purpose,
    for nothing can thwart love.
Amen.

Luke 4.31-37

You made your mark again, Jesus of Nazareth,
    on another sabbath day.
Ordinary folk, long used to a diet of lifeless words
    from company men,
    were astounded and delighted by the way you spoke.
Your words were shocking,
    you disturbed the dark wind that blew
    in a greatly afflicted and crushed down man.
He felt you were trouble and he was doomed.
He used a barrage of words in an attempt
    to stem the influence of your presence,
    as though he could unmask your power
    by shouting your name.
But all you required was silence
    and the affliction was disembowelled and disempowered.
All you require from us is silence,
    as our words are often a defence
    to keep your presence and threat at bay,
    wrongly believing we are in control of our lives.
Help us to receive the authority of your utterances,
    spoken with few words, yet of great integrity.
Amen.

Luke 4.38-44

Home visitor, fever rebuker,
 you did your work, again on the sabbath,
 of repairing the damage we've sustained on the journey of life.
Your passion was to make things as they should be
 and not become the local boy made good,
 nor the demigod of the day.
So you hid your Messiahship and cloaked your Sonship
 as you surely knew they would be misconstrued
 and misunderstood.
Then, early, as the sun broke from beyond the horizon
 you made out for the quiet and deserted place.
Yet, even there, you were hunted down to prevent your
 journeying on.
But Lord, it is you who needs to prevent us.
Prevent us from drawing you back into our small worlds.
Prevent us from thinking our concerns are the most important.
Prevent us from imprisoning you in our life-sapping anxieties.
Give us a concern for your purposes
 which embraces folk beyond those sun revealing horizons.
Amen.

Luke 5.1-11

While you stood on the waters' edge, Lord Jesus Christ,
    people hungry for freshness and hope crowded in.
We too are hungry for freshness and hope
    but we do not always recognise our emptiness.
Instead, we busy ourselves with displacement activities
    of church and work and hobbies,
    as if these will save and heal us.
Putting out into deep water, the soon-to-be disciple fishermen
    were sceptical of the extent of your masterfulness.
But Peter was humbled and fearful;
    all were amazed once again at the extent of your mission.
As the men in boats heard your call, may we listen to your voice.
As they upped sticks and followed, may we not be reticent
    to leave our own much-loved projects to one side.
Amen.

Luke 5.12-26

Lord,
    in the city, you saw the humiliated man
    diseased, broken and excluded.
You chose to fulfil his wish, break his painful exile
    and free him from his prison of that infectious skin disease.
He received his wholeness, but the people saw a spectacle
    and gossiped the story around the neighbourhood,
    the story you wanted to keep under wraps.
So you withdrew to a quiet place.
Another time, some pernicious religious leaders
    came to watch you from a distance
    as they wished to protect their advantage and vested interests.
You proved your authority to forgive sins
    by banishing a man's paralysis.
The people were amazed,
    they had seen strange things that day
    and the watching religious men retained their scepticism.
Keep us from having closed hearts and minds.
Inspire us to call out to you
    for our freedom.
Lead us to the deserted place,
    without fear.
Amen.

Luke 5.27-32

Travelling Jesus, moving on from watching religious cynics,
    you saw Levi: tax collector, low life, imperial collaborator,
    extortioner and sinner.
Your words were few, direct and loving, "Follow me."
Bound together by their solidarity of exclusion,
    all Levi's spurned work friends gathered
    for his joining-up party.
We also watch and judge and tut-tut
    when we see who you include;
    while not called scribes and Pharisees,
    we act as if we are religiously elite.
Contrary to our ways, you bind people together
    by your solidarity of inclusion: of the sinner;
    the outcast; those beyond the pale; and the unforgiven.
Like wine buffs, we like to think old and vintage is best.
Open our hearts and minds to all the new you offer
    which is fresh, life-giving and old-ways destroying.
Amen

Luke 5.33-39

Lord of all,
    help us to sense the times and the seasons of our faith,
    when to celebrate, rejoice and party,
    and when to take time out to prepare and fast.
Keep us from restricting our practice
    to simple formulas or narrow dogmas,
    for your life is varied, rich and usually unpredictable.
Keep us from holding onto what is past
    when it is only because of our nostalgia.
Keep us from patching up old ways of church
    that no longer carry the mystery.
Keep us from ruining your newness
    by refusing to let go of what is past.
Your ways of acting in the world are vastly different from ours;
    stop us from making wrong compromises
    which only destroy your Spirit's vital work.
Amen.

Luke 6.1-11

On yet another sabbath, Lord,
    you provoked a further controversy
    by allowing your men to do what was not deemed legal,
    according to the bylaws in the Pharisees' little book.
They picked some seeds from the crop in the field
    as they passed through
    and having eaten it, you stood accused and condemned.
Your rebuttal was simple and straightforward,
    "The Son of Man is lord of the sabbath."
And then on yet one more sabbath occasion,
    in the place of congregation,
    you challenged your sceptical religious minders
    about what good is permissible from their little book of rules
    on such days.
Is it good to do good? Is it good to harm?
Is it good to save a life? Is it good to destroy a life?
But their anger and indignation soared
    and they plotted what they might do with you.
We get angry too in our self-righteousness
    with our many self-justifications.
But help us to seek the good
    and not protect our own sense of superiority.
Amen.

Luke 6.12-16

This time Lord you did not go to the desert to pray,
    but to the mountain.
You went into the darkness of the night to see more clearly.
And then you called "apostles", those to be sent.
You changed one man's name.
You took on hot-headed brothers.
You invited the boy with the Greek name.
You embraced a political rebel.
You chose a tax collector – a sinner by default.
You appointed a character
    who one day would become your traitor.
You selected another who would not believe unless he first saw.
You commissioned some of whom we know nothing.
You called a hotchpotch mixture
    that no sane strategist would engage.
And you call us too:
    some full of fear;
    some unsure and paralysed by doubt;
    some wracked with guilt;
    some who feel they have nothing to offer;
    some broken, seemingly beyond repair;
    some who have deeply wronged and hurt others;
    some marginalised and stigmatised by outwardly decent people.
You call many who feel they have no right to be called,
    and that's how you call us.
The big issue for us is this: Will we have the courage to follow?
Amen.

Luke 6.17-19

No longer out in the desert or up on a mountain, Lord,
   you stood on a flat place to speak plainly.
Disciples, apostles and people from near and far
   travelled for your wisdom and wholeness-making touch.
Some had journeyed for days, some had never been
   so far from home.
And this time you did not disappoint,
   except for those who had much to lose.
The energy and the power came out of you
   and yet you were not diminished in love or strength.
We want a thirst for deep wisdom.
We want to hear the hidden message
   which is invisible to powerful people.
We want to sense your presence,
   without which we will never be whole.
Amen.

Luke 6.20-26

Jesus, you say to us:
    look up my friend,
    the new regime belongs to those who are poor;
    look up my friend,
    starving people will be full with food;
    look up my friend,
    as you have wept, so now you will roar with laughter;
    look up my friend,
    hated and excluded people will eventually win out.
But look out, you who are wealthy,
    your supply will be cut off.
And look out, you who are self-indulged and full,
    one day you will feel the hunger pangs of others.
And look out, you with your mocking derisory laugh,
    in the end, you will grieve and cry in sadness.
And look out you who everyone applauds,
    celebrities often come to a sticky end.
Amen.

Luke 6.27-38

O God, we do not like our enemies.

We fear people who hate us.

We do not want to spend time with those who curse us.

We avoid those who are violent and all who rob from us.

And yet you call us to love them, to be good to them,
    to pray for them, to give to them and be generous to them!

We cannot, though, avoid your golden rule,
    "Do to others as you would have them do to you."

We prefer to take the comfortable route of sticking close
    to those we like
    and those who are like us.

In this, you say, there is no reward, no benefit.

We can cope maybe with the challenge of loving our neighbour,
    but loving our enemy does not come naturally to us.

Teach us the lesson of mercy.

Show us the payback of living with generosity
    written throughout our lives.

Then we will have no need to be superior.

Then we will not feel the need to protect our reputations.

Then we will see how much has been given to us.

Then we will know what is given is also received.

Amen.

Luke 6.39-49

O God, we loathe to be labelled hypocrite,
    for our self-image is so much higher than this.
We believe it is others who are blind to themselves,
    but we delude ourselves
    as we are sightless too – so come, heal us.
Our fruit is often bad,
    yet we cannot smell its rottenness.
Help us to treasure in our hearts all that is good and wise
    and generous,
    as out of this you will bear good fruit.
We speak as though we believe in our hearts,
    but we act as if we live in disbelief.
We do not want our lives to be washed away at their foundations
    when hard times come
    and suffering challenges our shallowness.
Come, help and heal us,
    as we cannot help ourselves while alone.
Amen.

Luke 7.1-10

O Great Compassion,
    detach us from our prejudices
    so we may see the good in all people,
    especially among those we view as enemies of our faith
    or our interests.
Detach us from our preconceived ideas
    that it is only those who are part of our group
    who can hold the truth and be part of your people.
Detach us from our made-up minds
    and the simple assumptions we make about other people
    because of their outward appearance, political loyalty,
    ethnic background or sexual preference.
We thank you for Jesus who sees through our ways
    and gives time and attention to those
    we would otherwise dismiss
    as undeserving of attention,
    or even cruelly term "a waste of space".
We thank you for the unexpected, non-religious people of life
    whose faith surpasses our own,
    even when they do not have the correct vocabulary
    to back it up.
We thank you, that you only have to speak the word
    and we too will be healed.
Amen.

Luke 7.11-17

O Life Lover,
    it is always sad when a young man dies ahead of his mother
    especially when she has also suffered
    the disgrace of widowhood.
The lamenting, impacted neighbourhood
    helped this broken woman carry her son and her grief.
O Life Lover,
    you too are not left compassionless when faced with such pain
    and devastation.
Your words, "Do not cry," seemed inappropriate to us
    until you stepped forward and touched the young man's coffin
    that carried him to his grave.
O Life Lover,
    we easily become shaken
    when you disrupt the way things routinely happen,
    even when you raised this young man from his demise.
But still, we want to see signs of your life among us,
    restoring sons to widows,
    restoring confidence to communities
    and giving hope to people like us,
    for we still want to believe
    that the era of the prophet is not yet over.
Amen.

Luke 7.18-35

Like John the Baptist, we also expected you, O Promised One,
    to judge us,
      but your pattern of relating is not what we anticipated.
You come to restore broken people, trodden down
    by the affairs of life
    and left destitute
    when others have taken more than their fair share.
May we still see the face of the prophet in the scruffy outsider
    who lives on the side of the street
    and whose words are written on subway walls.
May we still see the face of the prophet
    in the one who refuses to conform,
    who will not be caged into our controlling ways.
May we still discover those
    who, by their clarity of sight,
    can reveal things yet unseen to us.
May we not be like fickle young people,
    distracted by their own complaining,
    but like true children who are still able to wonder
    and live in awe.
Amen.

Luke 7.36-8.3

O Great Companion,[7] sharing bread at others' tables,
  you allowed shamed people to love you
  and adore you.
The ill afforded act of a despised woman
  said more to you than all of the pomp, prestige and ceremony
  of Simon the Pharisee.
Her kissing, her weeping, her bathing and her drying of your feet
  with her careful anointing,
  said more than a thousand so-called righteous acts.
We too are appalled at times when outsiders
  do not play by the rules,
  when others ruin the decorum of polite society
  and our self-styled respectful worship.
May we learn sombre Simon's difficult lesson;
  the one for whom little is forgiven, loves little.
May we be brave enough to love audaciously
  and, in so doing, know our sins are forgiven.
You have saved us, may we now go in peace.
Amen.

---

[7] A companion literally means one who shares bread with another.

Luke 8.4-15

O Rabbi,
    the wisdom-starved crowds tracked you down
    to seek insight and receive hope.
You served food of the word of life to them in stories,
    actions and teachings.
Some did not take root because of the cares of life.
Some did not take root because of the pressures of life.
Some did not take root because of the distractions of life.
Some did take root and the reason was clear for many to see.
We too are susceptible to the various winds of life
    which take us away from our true direction
    and consume us in fruitless activity.
We easily submit to these diversions
    so we might have a fleeting feeling of significance
    and importance.
Help us to hear from an honest and good heart,
    and with patient endurance
    so we become the people you meant us to be:
    goodness for the world we inhabit.
Amen.

Luke 8.16-21

Lord of all light
　　keep us from timidity,
　　for it hides the radiance
　　you have placed within us.
As we see by the brightness that shines on us
　　and from within us,
　　may others also see by that same illumination
　　so nothing remains hidden in darkness or secrecy.
As we listen, give us mindful attention
　　that we may hear more
　　than we first expected or hoped;
　　we do not wish to become deaf
　　like the many who refuse to listen.
Thank you for including us
　　in amongst your nearest and dearest,
　　for we too desire to obey your words.
Amen.

Luke 8.22-25

O Lord,
    it seems to us you are often asleep
    when we most need you;
    we call on you, but you don't respond.
Please come and rebuke the chaos of our lives
    and the turmoil of our world
    when we find it easy to blame someone else
    for all we see going awry.
Sometimes we feel we are perishing
    rather than growing in wholeness.
Sometimes we feel the world
    with its politics, economics and ecology only gets worse,
    without any hope of improvement.
So we shout to you, "Master, Master!"
    and we hear you say, "Where is your faith?"
We have to admit our faith has melted away
    in the troubles and sufferings of life.
Come and act in our world and in our lives
    that we may be amazed
    and even a little afraid.
Amen.

Luke. 8.26-39

O Liberator,
we pray today for all who are seriously dehumanised:
    for those far from home without a place to rest;
    for street people who have no one to belong to;
    for all possessed and dispossessed;
    for the tormented and abused; and
    for the many who have become sick in spirit, soul,
    mind and body as a result of living
    without community.
For many, you have become a frightening destabiliser
    who threatens the little security they grasp onto in life.
For others, religion has become a negative denying power
    rather than a liberating energy,
    resulting in a harvest of suspicion and mistrust.
Powers and prejudices of society and culture
    have demonised and scapegoated
    those who are vulnerable or different.
Even though it causes great disruption to our ordered ways of life,
    come, heal and deliver the afflicted,
    come, expose the vulnerability
    of those who hold excessive power,
    come, restore humanity for individuals and neighbourhoods.
Amen.

Luke 8.40-56

Incurable illnesses and impending death
    haunt us through the various phases of our journey.
O life-giver Lord,
    you interrupted your urgent call
    to the dying, only child of a community leader.
You allowed yourself to be distracted
    by an unnamed, unknown woman with a chronic condition
    which did not immediately threaten her life.
This woman, amongst the lowest of the low,
    was not marginal to you, though,
    but a person of great faith.
You did not prioritise the influential, the celebrity
    or the most important,
    over those unseen and unclean, for all are children of God.
A child's life was saved,
    a woman's exile was ended and communities were restored.
Today, heal children who are dying,
    lift women who are sick and trodden down
    by prejudice and abuse
    and heal us as a people
    as we live alongside and together with each other.
Amen.

Luke 9.1-9

O Christ, call us.
Call us to what you want us to be,
    as people and as communities.
Call us to what you want us to do, alone or with others.
Call us, for we are marked out as baptised people.
Remind us, that to start serving you we need:
    no special qualification or training;
    no particular equipment or technology;
    no building, organisation or a strapline;
    all we have to do is begin.
Teach us how to live as good news to others
    more by who we are than by what we say.
Teach us how to be transforming agents
    in amongst the mix of people we encounter in our homes,
    at the local shops or around our workplaces.
Teach us the simplicity of being healers
    in a world immersed in pain and hell-bent on destruction.
At the same time, perplex the minds of leaders
    and powerful influencers
    when they see ordinary people living your new economy
    of love, forgiveness and justice.
May they seek out the wisdom of humble people
    who have learnt to inhabit your mind.
Amen.

Luke 9.10-17

We yearn to be taken aside away from the noise of life
 and the shallowness and popularism of social media.
It seems the cacophony of life follows us
  to most places we travel to,
  and our digital networks prove inescapable.
Take us to quiet places, as you took your disciples.
The crowds are relentless in their neediness and insistences.
We grow weary with our compassionate acts
  when our resources run low.
We wish to turn our backs on the demands of life, of church,
  of oughts and shoulds
  and escape to lonely places.
Sometimes, though, when we are run dry by life,
  you ask us to show mercy one more time.
Teach us how to give in such situations
  and find what the crowd still has to offer.
Then, together, we will find limitless nourishment
  and not exhaustion
  in your presence.
Amen.

Luke 9.18-27

We do not fully understand who you are.
At times you are the God we worship.
At times you are the teacher we seek to obey.
At times you are the dying, crucified one.
At times you are a mystery to us all.
O Jesus Christ, may we see you for who you are
    rather than who we want you to be.
Stop us from forming you in our image
    which removes from you your potency and challenge.
Destroy our domesticating urge to limit and restrict
    your nature and person.
May we take time to absorb the truth that you are
    the Son of Man,
    the Suffering One, Man of Sorrows,
    rejected by those who think they are significant and important.
May we not talk about what we do not understand
    nor explain you and your mystery away
    in simplistic soundbites.
Instead, may we learn how to follow in your footsteps slowly
    and understand carefully what it means
    to take up our cross daily;
    we do not want to lose the one most important thing of life.
Amen.

Luke 9.28-43a

Take us up, Lord, into the mountains
    to the vantage point from where we see differently,
    the place of separation from business as usual.
We need to know more of you,
    more than merely spotting the hidden signs of your presence
    in the ongoing events of each and every day.
Root us afresh in the Great Tradition of Moses and Elijah,
    and the prophets of old, both women and men.
Root us thoroughly in our heritage
    so we have confidence for our future,
    even when we are weighed down by heaviness and sleep.
But keep us from creating mausoleums and monuments
    in which to imprison you and the Great Tradition.
As you lived the pattern of death and resurrection
    help us to imitate the same,
    as we too are chosen daughters and sons.
Teach us not to talk too easily about things we cannot fathom
    including our experience of participation in you,
    but nevertheless, may we still be liberators
    for those oppressed by things seen and unseen.
Amen.

Luke 9.43b-50

O Son of Man,
    your words are sobering to our ears
    and beyond our comprehension;
    we are afraid to ask for clarification.
But you speak clearly to us in images,
    above all in the image of a little child
    in whom we can see the face of God
    and encounter your mystery.
If such a small child is among the greatest
    in your management of life,
    then stop us from competing and comparing
    to see who is the better
    or which church is bigger, brighter or more successful.
Teach us to be open to those altogether different to us
    who also work for the good of all and creation
    and not build walls or barriers because of this difference.
Give us humble hearts and quiet spirits.
Amen.

Luke 9.51-62

Entering the end game,
    you travelled to your fate through the despised territories
    of mixed-race rejected peoples
    who were suspicious of your intentions
    and unwelcoming of your presence.
We, like your disciples, easily turn against all
    who do not receive you
    or are cautious towards you,
    without first listening to their story
    or entering their journey of religious pain and prejudice.
Like your followers, we make comments
    that increase their sense of isolation and exile
    and place them even further from your remit.[8]
Like so many religious people
    we prefer you to judge others rather than us.
We say we will follow you,
    but we have our "jobs to do" list of tasks
    we must first complete.
We swear unswerving allegiance to you
    but say we will enact our promises tomorrow.
Teach us how to let go *now*
    without fear of losing what we wrongly think is essential.
As you lead, teach us to follow.
Amen.

---

[8] The Samaritans were not considered to be part of God's people by the Jews as they were mixed race. Jesus, however, included them.

Luke 10.1-20

Lord, there is much to do and not many of us to do it.

But still, send us out into uncomfortable and dangerous territories
   which are not good for our image, our reputation or our ease.

We feel under-resourced and in need of some kindly distraction
   as we go on our way.

You ask us, however, to be single-minded,
   follow your lead and fulfil our vocation.

Change us, so wherever we may go
   others may sense peace travels with us,
   a resource that cannot be expended or taken from us.

Keep us from being shallow, jumping from job to job.

Stop us from being choosey or coveting others' callings.

Make us a gift to all we encounter,
   so we bring wholeness not injury.

May we not take it personally when folk think us strange
   or reject us,
   help us instead to dust ourselves down and not judge,
   as this is not our task.

May people see in us your face.

May people hear in our speech your words.

May people experience from us your loving compassion.

Remind us, we are already loved and named by you.

Amen.

Luke 10.21-24

Mother and Father God,
>   you have not done what we expected;
>   you have chosen an odd set of people:
>   misfits, infants and naive folk.
It is they, however, who can see more clearly
>   what it is you are getting at.
They can handle mystery better than those of us
>   who prefer logic and certitude over faith.
The bright, quick, well-read and sharp people
>   have been left out of the frame.
All things now exist in Christ.
You and Christ are one.
You and the Spirit are one.
We want to be fortunate,
>   so help us to see what these lowly folk see
>   and hear what they hear,
>   as this is the essence and the core of all reality.
Amen.

Luke 10.25-37

Teacher,
 we all like to receive a legacy.
What you offer, though, is not ours by right or inheritance,
 it is entirely gift.
So teach us how to fulfil your law of love:
 by how we love from the heart;
 by how we love from our souls;
 by how we love with our strength;
 and by how we love by using our minds,
 because we want to live fully.
Keep us from our mind games
 whereby we determine that some folk are unworthy of love.
Keep us from our hostility towards those we deem
 a danger to our much-valued faith.
Keep us from our fear of those who look different to us
 or whose traditions and festivals are not our own.
Keep us from passing judgement
 on those we have not bothered to get to know or love.
Instead, make us merciful and compassionate people
 so we even surprise ourselves
 by our acts of generosity.
Amen.

Luke 10.38-42

We behave as a frenetic people in your service,
    distracted by the many things we feel we should do for you
    and diverted from the few you really require of us.
Our lives are choked by our worries and anxieties
    and used up by our never-ending business and busyness.
May we, like Martha, become great welcomers and receivers
    of those who pass through our lives,
    offering the hospitality of home, food and rest.
May we also be like Mary, able to sit with our guests,
    not only to hear what they are saying
    but to listen to what is said.[9]
During this day,
    help us to receive you into the passage of the hours.
During this day,
    help us to hear you from beyond and behind
    the noise of our activity.
During this day,
    help us to find moments to sit and be present,
    attentive for the only necessary thing.
Then who we are and what we do
    will be transformed out of all recognition
    and the world will be impacted by life that has no bounds.
Amen.

---

[9] Hearing and listening are not always the same thing.

Luke 11.1-13

Lord, we do not know how to pray.
Some of us pretend we can.
Some of us beat ourselves up because of our inadequacy.
Whenever we come to you for friendship, acceptance and love,
    help us to realise we are knocking on an open door.
But teach us what the only necessary things of life are
    and what is ultimately most important
    so we do not end up chasing others' false dreams
    or our own fantasies.
Most of all, good God,
    we want your Spirit of Life, without which we are dead;
    then we will be nourished by your nurturing.
By living in your life-flow,
    may we be so free from the shame of our cock-ups,
    incompetences and rebellions
    that we may have sufficient generosity
    to let others off the hook,
    thus remaining secure in your management of our lives
    and this universe.
Amen.

Luke 11.14-28

O Jesus, great commander of things which frighten and scare us,
    of things hidden and threatening.
Your power over evil is sourced in love
    and your passion for justice is rooted in mercy.
Deal with our misuse of might
    and the times we have aligned ourselves with corruption
    rather than seeking truth and goodness.
Heal and deliver all those we have made victims
    through our scheming manipulations
    and bring them relief from their sufferings.
Show us there is only one way to deal with the evil
    in our midst
    and that force or personality or organisation
    cannot replace or replicate the strength of your loving humility.
Let us, then, not be a divided people
    or deliberately work against your grain,
    for nothing else can fill the void of our lives.
Our participation in these things
    is more precious to you than even your mother's love.
Amen.

Luke 11.29-32

You were not impressed when crowds turned out to see you,
　　but we love to see people come
　　in their hundreds and thousands.
You escaped the mobbing masses,
　　but we love to have our buildings packed to the gunnels
　　with ever-growing congregations, meetings and programmes,
　　even though this is often a vain and misplaced love.
All you offered that day was the sign of Jonah,
　　your primary sign of transformation.
However, this is not the news we want to hear
　　for we too want to run away from such speech.
We are people who break away from you and your liminal places
　　chasing instead our own dreams and delusions of grandeur,
　　looking for impressive signs and wonders
　　and not your death and resurrection mystery miracle.
We rarely go freely into the belly of the beast
　　as we prefer clear, easy and comfortable answers,
　　yet we know these dark spaces are our teachers.
So when we do submit,
　　we will in time be spat up on a new shore
　　to see and understand our call and purpose.
Lord, have mercy on us.
Amen.

Luke 11.33-36

O Light of the World
   you call us to be beacons of hope and love,
   so come and wash us until we shine.
We will repent,
   not simply to be better-behaved people
   but to be those who see more clearly,
   for then we will live as bright Jesus-shaped people.
Teach us to be truly attentive to the world
   in which you have placed us,
   keeping us from our addiction to the attention economy.
Help us to see things for their own value and worth,
   not just their usefulness to our self-centred projects.
Restore in us that first way of innocent-looking
   we lost so many years ago through our wounding.
Clean the lens of our souls
   that your light may shine in us and through us
   for our sake and everyone's sake.
Amen.

Luke 11.37-54

Like the religious rulers of old
    who liked to separate themselves from others,
    we too are overly conscious of how other people view us;
    our outward deeds are more obvious
    than the state of our inner lives.
Your repeated "woes" scare and offend us
    as we know we do not have our house in order.
Getting inconsequential detail right
    overrides our concern for justice and the love of God.
The status, security and size we covet for our churches
    twists our motives for mission and action.
We are unaware of our duplicitous actions
    and our compromised principles.
We do not realise the heavy spiritual burdens
    we place on those already bowed down.
So send us some prophets;
    open our ears to listen to them
    as we do not wish to suffer judgement.
Keep us from being a blockage or hindrance for others
    who would otherwise enjoy your great goodness.
May we not be hostile when prophets tell us things
    we would rather not face up to,
    so we too may be saved.
Amen.

Luke 12.1-12

Lord, we know we are each just one among billions
    and we fear our lives count for little
    in the grand scheme of things,
    but you notice and value each of us.
In our fragility, we aspire to be like others
    who seem more prominent, more successful
    and more influential.
But stop us from selling our souls
    by trading in hypocrisy
    (a trait we usually only recognise in others),
    for your, "Nothing is covered up that will not be uncovered,"
    frightens us,
    as our exposure would be long and painful.
May we be people of integrity,
    having inner lives that are congruent with our outer lives.
Only then will we easily stand before you and others.
Only then will we easily answer charges made against us
    as what we say will be guided by your life within.
Only then will we easily speak without hidden agendas,
    having no public image to protect.
Only then will we easily walk confidently
    into life with your Spirit,
    assured of our part in your greater Life.
Amen.

Luke 12.13-21

We live in a culture of greed
    and an economy fuelled by covetous advertising,
    enticing us to commit the last of your great commandments.
We are so immersed in this mindset we do not see our own sin
    or recognise our addiction to acquiring.
Building up our ever-growing portfolios
    (so we can relax, eat, drink and be merry)
    has become our song.
We have prioritised our private gain over the common good
    and made a mockery of your neighbourly manifesto.
We live as if what we own and how we are seen by others
    is the true essence of our lives and our total worth.
Teach us what makes us who we really are
    and what is most valuable,
    for then we will turn from our self-preoccupied ways
    towards our neighbours and our enemies.
Amen.

Luke 12.22-31

We are born worriers, Lord.
We ruminate and chew over matters for hours
    taking us away from the sacredness
    of the present moment.
You see, we believe life *is* mainly about food,
    clothing and possessions.
Teach us from your life as expressed in the birds of the air,
    the animals of the land, the fish of the sea
    and flowers of the field.
Even our great public heroes and media-soaked celebrities
    in all their finery
    do not possess the grandeur of these.
We worry your life does not adequately fill our being
    because we do not recognise you in the God-full life around us.
So help us to see differently.
Make us attentive to what we normally pass over in familiarity.
Open our eyes to your presence-filled world,
    and to see the fabric of creation
    as something more than a resource for us to exploit
    or profit from.
While the world is hell-bent on striving for what is not the best,
    may we not be counted among their number.
Amen.

Luke 12.32-48

Again, you teach us about the true treasure of life;
    you clearly believe we are slow to be convinced
    of your radical reality-changing agenda.
According to your teaching,
    our hearts are in our bank accounts
    and our aspirations
    are committed to an ever-improving lifestyle.
You require us to let go,
    to let go of our attachments to all that bogs us down
    and keeps us imprisoned on the treadmill of life.
You require us to be ready for your coming
    that happens today, tomorrow, in the future
    and at the end of time;
    we miss your daily coming when we are engrossed
    in an acquisitive-centred life.
Teach us from the blessed little people
    who live in freedom and are therefore able to see your coming
    today, tomorrow and every day.
Then we will treat others with kindness and consideration
    and not demand from them what they are not able to offer.
Then we will live contented and fulfilled lives.
Amen.

Luke 12.49-59

O fire-raging Lord,
    who brings division, not peace,
    who upsets happy families
    and comes to destroy rather than build;
    how can we deal with such texts which are an embarrassment
    to conventional faith?
How do we repeat the refrain today, "Thanks be to God"?
But your talk of fire is different from our talk of fire;
    your fire comes to clean and cleanse
    and prepare the ground for new growth.
Your talk of fire falls on the heads
    of believers at the Pentecostal party.
Your talk of fire is not our talk of fire.
We, though, want you to be
    the well-contained fire of our domesticated hearths
    and our mechanised boilers.
We want your fire to warm us in our smug self-satisfaction
    without upsetting our longstanding assumptions, prejudices
    and injustices.
We want the depths of humanity to remain untouched,
    leaving us just as we were, yet more peaceful.
But instead change us, for this is what we need.
Through our painful conflicts, reveal what has to burn in us.
Show us that the peace of Christ does not come to bring quietness
    and compliance,
    but an unsettling justice that puts all things right.
Amen.

Luke 13.1-9

We live, Lord, in a world
    where evil acts are perpetrated by man on man
    and where random acts and flukes of nature cause death
    and destruction.
We are prone as religious folk to blame other people
    for their poverty, their hunger
    or their misfortune.
Help us see our lives are fragile
    and our existence delicate
    so we then take stock of our lives
    and become mindful of where we have wrongly invested
    and banked our lives.
We do not know when the day or the hour will come.
We do not know when our lives will come to an end
    or when creation itself will find its fulfilment in Christ.
Make us ready, awake and alert for your coming.
Amen.

Luke 13.10-17

O Christ,
> you did not ignore the plight of women as others did
> nor place their needs and healing below the priority
> of obeying religious rules.

Come into our lives to rearrange our carefully chosen hierarchies
> of importance
> and lead us out of our conceit.

Lead us out of our stubborn resistance to your change
> to a compassion that sees beauty and potential for restoration
> in the most unlikely places.

May we have a healthy scepticism towards religious leaders
> and recognise they too are broken and fallen people.

May we act in obedience to your great law
> to enhance life with your great compassion
> wherever we may encounter it,
> so we may see an end to suffering and oppression,
> and rejoice with all who are liberated.

Amen.

Luke 13.18-21

O God,
    there is a wild exuberance about your way of doing things,
    and a carefree generosity that seems to be reckless
    and lackadaisical.
Wild creatures and underserving people
    take advantage of your big heart,
    taking what they did not work for.
Help us to see any small acts of kindness and open-handedness
    as valid expressions of your life and love among us.
The world needs big and powerful expressive acts
    to get its imperial designs established,
    but your kingdom works in smallness,
    the unlikely
    and the so-called undeserving.
Help us to look and see
    so we do not frustrate your life
    that flows between us,
    as our ways are not always your ways.
Amen.

Luke 13.22-30

We are back, Lord, to that old conundrum of yours:
    "Some who are last will be first,
    and some who are first will be last."
We like to know who is saved and who is not saved.
We like to think it is only us, the in-crowd, who will make it,
We like to be clear about who will not be included,
    about who will be last.
But you do not give in to our speculations
    or respond to our guessing games.
You challenge us to be ready.
Your hospitality is ample and generous
    but we live as though it will not always be available,
    or only available to some.
Help us to focus our attention
    so we remain aware and awake
    to the invitation into your presence,
    for without this we have nothing.
Amen.

Luke 13.31-35

O Jesus,
 as you set your face towards Jerusalem
 no threat of death deterred you from your objective
 or your liberating urge.
Pompous kings and men of the religious hierarchy
 could not distract you from your calling
 or make you water down your revolution.
As your heart was broken over your greatly loved capital city,
 give us a mother's love for all we see broken and misled.
Keep us from avoiding the tragic situations
 that people find themselves in,
 for through these we can find our path to wholeness.
We will not condemn.
We will not stand idly by.
We will not give up hope until we see you come.
Then we also will proclaim,
 "Blessed is the one who comes in the name of the Lord."
Amen.

Luke 14.1-14

We sometimes wonder, Lord, if the sabbath was your busiest day,
    healing the sick, challenging the privileged,
    provoking your followers.
Certainly, the sick went home healed
    while those who thought they had all the answers
    remained silent and speechless
    by entertaining you as a disruptive guest in their homes.
Of course, every day is a sabbath for you
    if there is an opportunity to distribute your diet of justice,
    restoration and love.
Teach us the mystery of your kingdom-reversing statement,
    "For all who exalt themselves will be humbled,
    and those who humble themselves will be exalted;"
    our temptation is to choose exaltation
    as we like to be well-regarded by others.
Show us how we can serve the poor, the paralysed, the lame
    and the blind
    as we see them amongst us,
    for in doing this we will be fortunate in serving you.
Amen.

Luke 14.15-24

Even though you were a guest at dinner
    you did not hold back from exposing patronising piety.
We too dish up a menu that often includes
    pie in the sky when you die,
    as if everything is to do with a distant future
    and nothing of the present.
But your reality is of this moment and for all people,
    especially the excluded.
So when we decline your invitation to participate
    in your economy of love today,
    you will circumvent us
    and reach directly to your much-loved people
    by hook or by crook.
We are surprised and shocked by your attitude to church
    and synagogue people,
    for if we will not work with you
    then you will work without us.
Turn our shock into mercy and our surprise into compassion,
    for the sake of the poor,
    for our sake
    and for your sake.
Amen.

Luke 14.25-35

O Jesus,
    who sought to escape the large crowds who pursued you
    over the miles you travelled,
    your call to hate our families and have no possessions
    makes us want to escape you, not seek you out.
But your loving/hating imperative,
    from your Semitic way of speaking,
    is your call for us to order our priorities correctly
    and not to turn our backs on all that is good in this world.
Teach us how to live your strapline message,
    "Whoever does not carry the cross and follow me
    cannot be my disciple."
Remind us how much it will cost us
    to travel with you;
    we do not want to set out on this journey
    only to fall by the wayside when life becomes too difficult.
Having said all this,
    we do want to make a difference in this broken world
    by living your salt-styled life in a manure[10] sort of way.
Amen.

---

[10] See v. 35.

Luke 15.1-10

The disreputable, the unmentionables and the forbidden
    crowded out your personal space
    and you revelled in their company,
    while those suffering from religionism
    stood at a distance and judged you.
Your proposition of leaving some folk
    in the danger of the wilderness alarms us.
    as we assumed all lives matter,
Clearly, some obdurately stand in opposition to you
    and you grant them their desire,
    to be left alone – truly alone, even in danger.
You party with those who know they are lost and far from home.
You delight in the minorities who embrace your invitation
    to go beyond the mind and enact your "metanoia",[11]
    for they realise this is how the true transformation
    of the heart truly happens.
To us, you are the roaming shepherd and the searching woman
    who looks and looks
    until you finally find such preciousness.
You are Jesus the tenacious,
    you are God the rejoicer.
Amen.

---

[11] The Greek *metanoia* means more than simply turning around, as it is often explained. It means "beyond-thought", with *meta* meaning "beyond" (as in the modern word "metaphysics") and *nous* meaning "mind" (as in the modern world "paranoia"). Jesus invites us to go beyond our usual mind-limiting thinking, for this is what will change the way we behave.

Luke 15.11-32

We confess Lord,
    like the profligate boy, we think what we have
    and what we enjoy is a given, not a gift.
We also take diversions on the journey of life
    to indulge our numerous ridiculous desires
    and demand our selfish expectations be fulfilled.
What surprises us is you allow us to go on such benders
    which endanger our lives and waste money and time,
    or you permit us to indulge in affairs
    that risk our relationships.
Just as you allow us to enter the belly of the whale
    so too you allow us to sink in the depths of the pigsty,
    as you know too well these are some of the few places
    where we'll open ourselves to your unbelievable,
    non-condemnatory embrace.
In this great acceptance is our hope and renewal.
Keep us from deep resentment, though,
    when we see others included,
    who we think should have made a greater effort
    at self-correction,
    for we too are in the same mire as them.
Amen.

Luke 16.1-13

Jesus,
    your talk of a rogue and dishonest manager
    leaves us scratching our heads.
We admire rich people,
    but you promise to send them away empty
    for they benefit from what they do not work for.
But we too are complicit within a system that benefits us
    at great cost to poor people and debt-laden nations.
Show us how to act creatively and concretely,
    and how to use our economic privilege
    to rebuild just, social relationships
    with those oppressed by the systems we benefit from.
May we proclaim the message that our culture, ruled by capital,
    is ultimately unstable and unsustainable.
Unlike poor folk, we Western Christians have a far greater choice
    about how to spend and deploy our financial resources
    than we are socialised to imagine.
Your subversive call to discipleship
    refuses to exonerate those of us
    neck-deep in the filthy rotten system.
Keep our responsibility to act strongly in our vision
    that we may use our wealth to rebuild community
    and establish justice.
Then we too will be well-regarded among our fellow humans.
Amen.

Luke 16.14-18

You alarm us, Jesus, when you say such things as,
  "What is prized by human beings is an abomination
  in the sight of God;"
  either you overstate your case
  or we under emphasise the radical nature of your calling.
We confess we regularly and repeatedly justify ourselves
  on so many matters in our vain hope to save face,
  but what you say confirms our instincts:
  you know what is in our hearts before we realise it.
We confess we have signed up to the world's mammon agenda;
  we do not know how to extract ourselves from it
  and also fear the prospect of doing so.
The power of your agenda is to be found in the Great Tradition
  and its adventurous, forward-looking inclusion
  of those we thought prohibited.
Teach us then to live in your post-Egyptian, post-empire,
  ten-fold Sinai agenda
  in fidelity and neighbourliness.
Amen.

Luke 16.19-31

You warn us, Lord, via this cartoon-styled story,
    that we too are people who luxuriate in great affluenza,
    overlooking the needs and rights of others.
When we clothe ourselves in fine cloth,
    cut to impress and stand out in the crowd above others,
    remind us that you will one day put all wrongs right
    and level up the exploitative biases of our society.
When we feed ourselves at the expense of the hungry
    with fine food,
    may we give ear to Moses and all the prophets
    who were clear and outspoken about systemic injustices.
Show us how we can live as disciples of Jesus
    who came to level things up
    and institute a new way of living within his new economy.
Then we can rest with Lazarus, intimate with father Abraham,
    and call ourselves "God is my help"[12] too.
Amen.

---

[12] Lazarus is derived from the Hebrew *El'āzār* (Eleazar) meaning "God is my help".

Luke 17.1-10

We stagger, crash and bumble our way through life
  causing much scandal in the process.
Help us wake up and become aware
  so we might not cause any of the "little people"
  to stumble or fall;
  it would be a better option for us to be thrown
  into the life-destroying ocean than for that to happen.
It seems we often believe we need something extra from you
  to prevent such failure and falling;
  we think we need more faith.
We have not yet realised it,
  but we already have enough of the faith stuff
  to uproot a worthless false fig tree[13]
  and plant it in life-destroying seawater,
  such is your resource within us.
Give us eyes to see those who are humble,
  vulnerable and open that we may learn from them
  and not distract them from the path.
At the same time, help us to identify the trees with false figs
  that offer only meagre nourishment to the poor and exploited,
  so we may have the courage and strength to cast these
  to their destruction,
  thus disempowering them of their power to maim.
This is our duty and our calling.
Amen.

---

[13] This tree has sometimes been referred as a "false fig" because from a distance it looks to be fruitful and delicious, but offers barely enough nourishment that only the poor would choose to eat.

Luke 17.11-19

You seemed to thrive, Lord, in borderland regions,
    the betwixt and between places,
    where untouchables lived and lodged
    far away from well-mannered society.[14]
On the final leg of your journey to the holy city,
    the fact of a miracle was eclipsed by the faith and gratitude
    of the foreigner among the outcasts:
    an outcast among outcasts.
Also remembering Naaman, the Syrian and the enemy,
    we are humbled by the attitude and conviction
    of many outside the church
    who do not call themselves Christians
    or class themselves as one of our number,
    but are nonetheless able to live in your Spirit
    of thanksgiving and forgiveness.
The scope of your mercy is scandalous
    and upsetting to our well-arranged worlds,
    but within this great economy of love rests our hope.
Amen.

---

[14] Victims of leprosy, or whatever skin condition this might have been, were exiled away from everyone else. This was according to the law, but conveniently away from well-to-do people. Jesus did not avoid such people he met on the road.

Luke 17.20-37

Men in power wanted to know when your regime was coming,
   assuming it could be observed, measured and evaluated.
It cannot, though, be subjected to such scrutiny,
   only experienced and embraced.
Over the years many had promised its arrival
   but as you insist, it is already here among us,
   within us and around us.
So we will not go chasing rumours or idle dreams
   but live the reality already present to us.
For your regime, you paid a high price;
   keep us therefore from being addicted to the possessions
   and aspirations of each and every day,
   otherwise we too will be in danger of missing the final greatness
   when it comes.
Make us ready for your sudden and unexpected arrival
   when you come to us, O Son of Man.
Amen.

Luke 18.1-8

O God,
    give us a shameless audacity
    to persist in pressing for what needs to be righted.
You do not speak in oxymorons
    or act in the perverse ways of unjust judges.
Give us faith to hope and pray and act
    in a world dominated by powers which respect no-one:
    not God; not people; nor communities.
Make us unusual in holding out against the odds
    and being annoyingly tenacious in fighting
    for social, racial and climate justice,
    especially for those who have been denuded the most.
Inspire us by the example of those who have fought
    seemingly unwinnable battles
    in the face of unreasonable and violent opposition.
May our churches recover "prayer-as-agitating-faith"
    so we become a pain in the neck
    to those who wield power without principle.
Amen.

Luke 18.9-14

So here we are again, meeting another of your oft-repeated,
    mind-bending, life-upsetting one-liners,
    "All who exalt themselves will be humbled,
    but all who humble themselves will be exalted."
You speak to all of us who trust in ourselves,
    who then easily slip into regarding others with contempt
    and derision
    because "we are not like other people".
You told the crowds, the least in the kingdom of God
    is greater than John the Baptist;
    this messes with our heads
    as this is just how things aren't in the real world.
In you we see the heart of God, in attitude of spirit:
    when you feasted and supped with Roman collaborators
    and dubious women;
    when you went out of your way to forgive their misdemeanours,
    while pointing out the greater sins of religious men.
Today you ask us,
    "Why do we fast, but do not see?"
    "Why do we act piously, but not notice?"
May we not stand alone as the self-absorbed pray'er did,
    but stand with those who are humiliated
    and discriminated against
    so we, in the spirit of our Great Tradition,
    help the oppressed go free.
Amen.

Luke 18.15-17

Not only do you seem to prefer disreputables and dodgy sorts
    as members of your gang,
    but you also suggest babies have a better idea
    about the things that concern you than we do!
Should your church be a babysitting service then?
Should we throw to one side all our carefully crafted protocols?
Should we dumb-down to the lowest common denominator?
It seems you go even further;
    we must become like them in some manner
    if we're to have a chance of attending your party.
It seems being "born again"[15]
    is not simply highly symbolic language or metaphor
    but there is some re-starting we must now learn to do.
It seems you were not joking when you tell us
    that your set-up has to be received
    as unmerited, unearned and unwarranted.
It is, for us, humbling that there is nothing we can do
    to win such status.
Amen.

---

[15] John 3.7.

Luke 18.18-30

We still do not get it:

    what you offer cannot be inherited,

    it is not ours by right,

    it is not ours by privilege,

    it is not ours by cultural association,

    it is not ours, until you freely give it.

Just because we have influence, it counts for nothing at all.

Just because we have position, status or role,

    they count for nothing at all.

Just because we have an exciting testimony to tell,

    it counts for nothing at all.

You give freely, simply because you are a care-free giver.

What we must do is to live your post-Egypt radical Sinai agenda,[16]

    living as people liberated from the constraints of any empire

    except the empire of your love.

Show us what the one thing is

    which keeps us imprisoned in the old mindset

    where we feel superior, entitled and self-justified

    for we cannot live with this and with you.

Amen.

---

[16] The Ten Commandments were not given as an arbitrary moral code, but as a radical alternative community model to the exploitative practices they had suffered in Egypt, the empire of the Pharaoh.

Luke 18.31-43

The destination of your journey was clear and purposeful;
    we travel, though, as those who are lost and blind
    with little idea or notion of what our days are for.
We struggle and languish for no good reason or benefit,
    tripping up over countless obstacles in our sightless lives,
    understanding nothing of our part
    in the great mystery of suffering and love.
So, Jesus, Son of David, have mercy on us
    and silence those who get in the way:
    those who think they have your best interests at heart;
    those who keep us from seeing and believing.
Remove our blindness
    that we may see as you see
    and not as we habitually do
    through our heavily tinted and biased lenses.
Join us with others who also beg for a better deal,
    for together we will live praise-filled lives
    and follow you on the road.
Amen.

Luke 19.1-10

Thankfully, your call to turn lives and assets around
    is not lost on every rich person.
The political and economic nature of your gospel,
    rooted in the age-old principles of jubilee and sabbath,
    are a call and challenge to all those of us in the affluent
    and well-heeled parts of the world.
It is no wonder wealthy people killed you;
    authorities that manage and wield power have a lot to protect
    and we have a history of executing prophets.
But this young man
    (whose short stature we sentimentalise
    to obscure your devastating message)
    is a sign of hope to all who feel trodden down
    and oppressed by sharks and extortioners.
If someone who had funded their lifestyle
    through theft and betrayal
    could be brought down from this high place,
    and if someone could be lifted up
    from their lowly destitute place,
    then the scope of your generosity has no bounds
    and the prophecy of Mary is true.[17]
So entice us to work for redistributive reparation
    so salvation can be seen in its fullest sense
    and not regarded as a private spiritual pick-me-up.
Amen.

---

[17] Luke 2.46-55.

Luke 19.11-27

We know, Lord, you are not a harsh master;
    you do not reap where you do not sow.
We know you do not bring people into your presence
    to be slaughtered.
We know you do not take from those who have little or nothing,
    giving it to those who have plenty.
We confess that for too long we have read this parable
    through the context of our competitive and acquisitive culture
    to which we are so attracted and attached.
Make us aware of the economic and political danger
    we live under and so often collude with.
Help us see it is those who are least able to resist
    (because of their poverty)
    who are exploited the most.
The saying is still true in our economic culture,
    "To all those who have, more will be given;
    but from those who have nothing,
    even what they have will be taken away."
Help us to warn others
    and work to build a way of living together
    that is just, kind, virtuous and non-violent.
Amen.

Luke 19.28-40

O Jesus, we mistakenly call your great piece of street theatre
   your "triumphal entry into Jerusalem".
We are shy of recognising it as a political and defiant action;
      it is easier for us to handle when we couch it in religious terms
      or spiritual language.
To admit that it is a non-violent defiant protest
      has severe implications for our own comfort and ease
      and threatens to overturn the tables
      of our own economic privilege and dominance.
You acted in protest against the status quo
      where a minority of the population enjoyed
      the majority of the wealth
      at the expense of the many.
We are not called to be people of revolt and unbridled anger,
      nonetheless, call us to be a people who have courage and guts
      in a world where brute force has had control for too long.
Call us to shout out against exploitation, oppression and injustice
      and then, maybe, others will shout about us,
      "Blessed are these who come in the name of the Lord!"
Amen.

Luke 19.41-48

O weeping Lord,
    we remember that other time when you cried
    by the side of your great friend's grave;
    sadness and broken-heartedness are not foreign to you.
Seeing a stubborn refusal to accept your alternative way
    of freedom living,
    while knowing the destruction such idiocy
    would inevitably lead to,
    is crushing even for the strongest heart.
Today, we still seem hell-bent on living the old story
    of idolising ever-growing wealth,
    fear of those who are different
    and the rejection of neighbourly, God-rooted living.
Come and shock us with your prophetic warnings
    before it is too late.
Show us how we have robbed resources from the marginalised
    and extracted cheap labour from the vulnerable,
    while making out it is all the fruit of your blessing.
Start a revolution in our hearts before it is too late
    and we end up destroying all you have gifted to us.
Teach us how to live in prayer
    and not rob from each other.
Amen.

Luke 20.1-8

Having caused a commotion in the public worship arena
    you then had the audacity and gall
    to return to teach in its precincts a few days later.
No wonder the "big guns" were on your back,
    challenging your reckless, incorrigible behaviour
    and questioning the legal basis for your prophetic action.
But like any great rabbi,
    you answered their questions with another question,
    for by this you get to the very core
    of their objections against you.
We too like cut and dried answers which put us on the right side
    and place our adversaries in the wrong.
However, you are not a God who can be defined by legalese
    nor the small print of fearful ruling men,
    for you are God who exists in the relationship
    of Father, Son and Holy Spirit.
So take from us our closed definitions
    and destroy our self-constructed boundaries
    that keep other people out,
    leaving them distant from us.
Amen.

Luke 20.9-19

We have often heard it spoken,
    "The stone the builders rejected
    has become the cornerstone."
But true to form,
    what we did not anticipate or notice
    has become the most important.
What we discarded as of no value has the highest value.
What we thought useless is, in fact, the most useful.
What we considered a hopeless way of doing things,
    is your subversive, anti-imperial way of doing things.
All we see and despise each day is crucial
    for your planet/people saving project.
Prompt and jar our memories about the age-old story
    in which you have repeatedly reaffirmed
    your choice of the outside, the bottom and the edge.
Take us back to this age-old wisdom
    so we do not follow the world's default setting
    of prioritising success, prestige, size and power.
Take us back to what your future is going to be.
Amen.

Luke 20.20-26

Slimy two-faced holy men followed you
    pretending to be honest and genuine in their interest.
They sucked up to you, but with one motive only – to trap you.
Because you were wise to their devious tricks,
    you again turned their question back on to them,
    in great rabbinic style.
In response to their deadly question of paying taxes
    to the occupying foreign power,
    you asked for a coin
    and so proved their collusion with the empire.
They carried imperial coins;
    they were already compromised.
They could not live separate lives
    from the exploitative Roman economy.
We are also compromised.
We also cannot live
    without dealing with abusive corporate powers.
Have mercy on us while we live in this uncomfortable,
    compromised gap.
Our lives are tainted by the spirit of empire;
    we collude with it on a regular basis
    simply to make our way through each day.
Help us to recognise everything ultimately belongs to you
    so we may bring more of it
    under your manner of operation.
Amen.

Luke 20.27-40

O Christ of Abraham, Isaac and Jacob,
    you do not invest yourself in dead people,
    for all are alive to you.
We have an immature upstairs-downstairs view
    of life beyond death;
    we do not live in a three-decker, flat earth set-up;
    we live in an integrated reality.
In "heaven":
    there will be no corner in eternity for my countrymen;
    there will be no place for my family to dwell alone;
    there will be no enclave for each
    of the different religious traditions.
Earth's reality will not be mirrored in heaven,
    for heaven's reality is mirrored here on earth.
In the resurrection,
    we will be closer to you than we are to our own breath.
In the resurrection,
    we will be closer to ourselves than we have ever been.
In the resurrection, we will be closer to all people
    than we have ever been to folk here on earth,
    for participation in your life
    has been your plan since the beginning of all creation.
In the resurrection, we shall all be in you, O Christ.
Open our shut eyes,
    so we no longer exist in our compartmentalised lives
    that keep us separated from others
    to preserve our illusory identities.
Amen.

Luke 20.41-47

Teach us to be wary of those who emphasise position and status,
    and cautious when people heap praise upon us,
      for we do not want to become re-embroiled
      in the seduction these have previously tempted us with.
Take us away from our counting of numbers
    and measuring the size of our so-called impact,
      for in doing this we are not looking to you,
      we are bolstering up our own flagging egos.
Instead, make us question prominent people
    as to what their reasons and motives are
      for parading their prestige and standing,
      and ask them why they need human evaluation
      of all they see happening to feel encouraged;
      it is as if they do not believe their names are written in heaven.
You are the called and chosen one
    who looks inferior to the mighty chosen ones of history
      yet who is nonetheless greater,
      for in your way of doing things
      the least are mightiest and the last are first.
Amen.

Luke 21.1-4

You recently busted down the doors of the Temple's fraud racket
   and opposed the religious class
   who act with great injustice
   to "devour the homes of widows" under the pretext of holiness.
For too long we have romanticised about this poor woman,
   because she placed "all she had" into the temple coffers.
We've held her up as a wonderful example of devotion and piety,
   just as we, as rich people, so easily sing,
   "What can I give him, poor as I am?"[18]
As we are able to give out of our abundance,
   we are blind to our affluent perspective
   and the robbery from the poor which keeps the rich wealthy.
She gave her legal requirement
   and left her children destitute and hungry;
   shame on the temple system that demanded and demanded.
While the moneyed
   can parade their large donations to multiple causes,
   (which remain only a fraction of what they,
   and we, already have),
   the poor have the little they have taken away.
Come, dismantle our systems which rob the poor,
   painful though it may be,
   and establish justice, here, in place of our over-extended piety.
Amen.

---

[18] Most people who sing this line at Christmas cannot really be classed as poor.

Luke 21.5-19

Despite your repeated encouragements
    for us to keep our cool with you,
    we need to talk about your worrying words
    for they frighten and dismay us.
Following your escalated series of conflicts with the authorities
    and your final dramatic exit from the Temple grounds,
    we enter your apocalyptic season of strife and difficulty.
Like your disciples,
    we are impressed by expensive and expansive buildings,
    and in awe of their grandeur and architectural wonders.
In the face of oppressive, dominant social institutions
    you come with your alternative vision,
    couched in a language that pushes us
    beyond our simple home-spun reasonings.
May we not be taken in by charlatans and spin doctors
    who come to tell us they have the words of hope
    when it is just another cycle of violence and theft.
Give us the backbone we need to stand up and be counted
    as an antidote to our addictive-compulsive binging
    that is pillaging the earth and taking us to the brink.
Keep us from being sucked into the fevered vortex
    of rumours and speculative explanations,
    for history and its unfolding is in your hands.
Amen.

Luke 21.20-24

O God,
 what we build will eventually fall
 unless it is built for your radical alternative way of living
 and from hearts of love.
Certainly, what we have fashioned with our hands
 to attract human praise and to impress,
 will come tumbling down
 as certainly as the walls of Jericho and Jerusalem fell.
As we have banked our wealth for the wrong purposes,
 we will be devastated by such great loss
 if we continue in this vein.
So break our long-held attachments to all that binds us
 to what is futile, self-serving and passing.
Give us the courage we need to leave behind
 all that gives us fleeting comfort
 and all that props up our susceptible fragile,
 self-made identities.
But even in our devastation, protect us and help us
 for we are sorely tested by our wayward
 and crooked ways of living.
O Lord, have mercy on us.
Amen.

Luke 21.25-38

O God,
  all things are subject to your timing and your purpose.
O Son of Man,
  all things are subject to your return.
We live in terrifying times and easily succumb to panic and doubt;
  it seems numerous threats surround us.
Some days it is hard to remain with hope for ourselves
  and our loved ones.
We are alarmed as a world community
  by violent minority groups,
  by how we have pillaged and raped the earth,
  and by the destructive power of our own industrial
  and military might.
We get confused by all these threatening events
  and ask if these are signs,
  but we are left unsure – yet we want to be sure.
We are sure that life as we know it will not always remain,
  and we are sure the day of your return (whatever that means)
  will bring an end to our plight of suffering and confliction.
In the meantime, hold us close and steady
  so we might remain alert and watchful
  and not be overcome by the troubles we see around us,
  nor the troubles we are part of.
Amen.

Luke 22.1-13

Your journey up to Jerusalem was long for many reasons,
    not least that you journeyed to your death.
With the crowds making their annual pilgrimage,
    you made your way to your inevitable conflict
    with corrupt politics and self-serving religion.
Power-brokers plotted your end,
    stealthily hidden from public opinion,
    with even one of your own, who had had enough
    of your lack of commitment to a violent-styled revolution,
    breaking ranks.
Behind the scenes, your furtive capture was plotted
    when money changed hands to seal the deal.
In the spirit of the Great Tradition of escape,[19]
    you planned your own secluded liturgy
    to celebrate the event of the flatbread
    that was uninterrupted, poignant, intimate and faithful.
So preparations were made and the stage was set
    for a drama that was not to be fictional in any way.
We will prepare ourselves to ensure we do not forget
    the mystery of your passion and love,
    and to anticipate our emancipation from subjugation
    with a minimum of words and busyness.
Amen.

---

[19] The Passover was a kind of party to celebrate national emancipation from that subjugation of old when the Children of Israel escaped from the slavery of Egypt under Moses.

Luke 22.14-23

So the stage was set, O Son of Man,
    and you took your place amongst your nearest and dearest
    for the meal you had carefully planned prior to your suffering.
These last actions before your end,
    taking, eating and drinking,
    were signs of deep solidarity among your followers
    and also with God's people of history.
But even in these vital, precious last moments
    when darkness was in your midst,
    you welcomed and embraced the betrayer
    before he went to earn his pieces of silver.
O Wine Producing Vine, O Bread of Life,
    your life was poured out for the sake of the world
    and your life is still poured out to us
    in this simple sacramental act.
Draw us into your embrace and imprint your passion on our lives,
    then we will be faithful to the great impulse of your love
    that has been energised
    and working since the foundations of the universe.
Then we will be counted among your number.
Amen.

Luke 22.24-38

In the build-up to the most powerful moment of your life
    your men argued about who was the most impressive
    and outstanding:
    about who was the best;
    about who was the finest.
As they jockeyed for position, power and popularity
    you immediately reminded them
    that this was exactly how the current political culture operated.
But your culture, however, is an upside-down, inside-out,
    youngest over greatest operation,
    where the least has the top position;
    those who sit at the top table are called to get off their thrones
    and wash the feet of others.
You have no interest in our games of competing and comparing,
    nor our parading of status, titles and honours.
Remind us we are fickle
    and liable to betray you at any moment;
    keep us humble and unpretentious.
Prepare us for the upset to come
    when what is familiar is taken away
    and what we thought treasure is lost.
In all this disruption, keep us non-violent and peaceable;
    may we never take up arms against those who oppose us.
Amen.

Luke 22.39-53

Following your habit and discipline
    you made your way out of the city
    and across the valley to your place of prayer,
    opposite the Temple which served as a den of thieves
    rather than a house of prayer.
Teach us what it means to wait, watch and pray.
Your prayer was a struggle between obedience
    and natural human need,
    where in honest and anguished speaking
    you fought the battle of the heart.
Teach us how not to let our attention drift
    when we should remain aware and present.
Teach us to move beyond our requisitive and needy prayers
    which leave us monitoring your rate (or success)
    at providing answers,
    or oblige us to make up explanations why some are not fulfilled
    to protect your reputation.
Teach us how to respond properly
    when attacks are made against us, verbally or physically,
    for we easily react with our destructive instincts
    instead of responding in love.
To our violence, you say, "No more!"
    there is enough already in the world and in our hearts.
Let us learn how to take up our crosses and follow you.
Amen.

Luke 22.54-62

Seized, captured, arrested, detained, questioned and interrogated;
    an experience for so many the world over.
We feel much like Peter;
    we can empathise with his reticent behaviour:
    following but fearful; concerned but uncommitted;
    visible yet in the shadows.
We feel the same way about many others who are
    seized, captured, arrested, detained, questioned
    and interrogated
    when no due legal process is followed
    and no economic justice is evident.
It is in the small things we renege on you, and others:
    by refusing to give a clear honest answer when questioned;
    by refusing to stand up for justice
    in the face of serious miscarriages;
    by refusing to step outside of our comfort
    and ease for the sake of another;
    by refusing to express our solidarity
    with those who suffer and have few options;
    by not remembering the Great Tradition or your teaching.
Sometimes we weep with sadness
    and sometimes our weeping is bitter,
    when we hurt more for ourselves than for you or others.
Turn our weeping into compassion
    and our denials into spoken truth
    for the sake of all.
Amen.

Luke 22.63-71

We humans can be incredibly cruel to each other,
    so incredibly inhumane:
    beating, persecuting and abusing prisoners.
Your full solidarity with us was nearing its completion
    as you stood before the so-called great and good
    who sat in pomp and ceremony behind the façade
    of being an appointed, legitimate group.
There is no response
    that will answer the jibes of your adversaries,
    no words that will settle the accusations of cynics.
Teach us when to speak and when to be silent.
Let us learn the wisdom of using our words carefully.
May we not be intimidated by the mockings of the many
    nor constrained by the tyranny of the masses.
To those who seek,
    you are the specially chosen one,
    and to those who search you are life.
Amen.

Luke 23.1-12

A three-fold charge was brought against you to the Governor,
    for which there was no evidence;
    your guilt had been determined.
But insistent people can grind down the most powerful of rulers,
    for they fear the crowds will turn against them.
Then a legal loop-hole was found;
    you were cast on the mercy of the local puppet king
    who wanted to see a spectacle, a sign from a wizard.
While vehement accusations and contemptuous mockings
    fell from the lips of those who stood and watched,
    you remained silent and still,
    enacting the advice of Moses to his people,[20]
    for the Lord our God fights for us.
As the God-chosen one,
    you were paraded that day in false royal attire
    while still no offence had been established.
As the power of evil was doubled that day and your fate sealed,
    enemies became friends.
You then moved closer to what you knew was necessary
    for the emancipation of the world
    and the removal of any reason to maintain enemies.
Amen.

---

[20] Exodus 14.14 says, "The Lord will fight for you, and you have only to keep still."

Luke 23.13-25

The Governor declared, "Not guilty!"
The King declared, "Not guilty!"
Yet still, a flogging was sentenced.
The gang leaders and the crowd shouted all the more loudly
    their distaste that you should live
    and called for the release of one guilty of stasis-revolt.[21]
They chose an activist
    convicted of a violent challenge to the powers-that-be
    in place of the activist convicted for non-violent love
    and a call for merciful justice.
Like Judas, they clearly thought you were not up to the job
    and preferred someone who could literally cut his way
    through the issues.
So, despite a third declaration of innocence,
    the rule of the mob was granted,
    a miscarriage of justice was enacted,
    the case was closed
    and your death assured.
Lord Jesus Christ, Son of God,
    have mercy on me, a sinner.
Amen.

---

[21] Luke here refers to Barabbas (Lit. "Son of the Father") as one involved in a *stasis*, a riot (Luke 23.19), one of the numerous attempted insurrections against Roman imperial power.

Luke 23.26-43

In good discipleship style, it was an outsider, a Libyan,
  who took up your cross along the way,
  and it was the women who remained to bewail your fate.
During such tragedy, you called for compassion for others
  as, if this could happen in a city when it is "in the greenwood",
  what on earth would happen when it is "dry"?[22]
As you entered the cranium place,[23]
  your exodus approached its climax
  and two convicted offenders were strung up alongside you.
Mindful of those who declared you guilty
  and announced the sentence,
  you spoke unbelievable words we cannot get out of our heads,
  "Father, forgive them,
  for they do not know what they are doing,"
  while the usual tradition of gambling
  for a dying man's few possessions took place at your feet.
Then, mocking instead of praise
  and sour wine instead of the new.
Inscribed in place over your head
  was the simple weighted statement,
  "This is the King of the Jews."
Remember us, Lord,
  for we do not wish to be counted among the dispossessed.
Amen.

---

[22] The sense of this is, "If this can happen in a time of relative peace (i.e. in the green), what on earth will happen when there is war or when the city is under siege (i.e. when dry)?"
[23] "The place called the Skull" (23:33), Luke used the Greek word for skull *kranion* from which we get cranium.

Luke 23.44-56

Such unusual happenings:
    darkness at midday in a Mediterranean country;
    human constructs of religious separateness
    ripped down the centre;
    and the loud haunting death-cry,
    "Father, into your hands I commend my spirit."
A chief among men became a worshipper and believer
    and droves of folk returned home full of sadness and regret,
    but the folk who truly loved you remained looking on.
Yosef, a council member from a provincial town
    and a true follower,
    bravely came forward to take your body
    and traded his grave so it might become yours,
    for he waited eagerly for your promise.
Only the women were left following to the burial site,
    returning home later with their anguish
    to prepare their spices and ointments.
Then it was sabbath in more ways than one.
Teach us to truly follow and not merely beat our breasts,
    for making all the right noises in the right places
    does not constitute discipleship.
Teach us to be like Yosef and the women.
Amen.

Luke 24.1-12

As dawn broke early on that morning, all was uncannily quiet.
There wasn't the razzmatazz, noise and drama
    we say happened on that life-changing, world-transforming day.
The women, who came silently to fulfil their burial duties,
    faithful as ever,
    found the grave broken open and devoid of any presence
    until two men, brightly attired,
    stood beside them in their perplexity.
Terror, dread and dismay pumped through their bowed bodies,
    when suddenly,
    "Why do you look for the living among the dead?
    He is not here, but has risen."
Remembering all you had said and predicted,
    Mary, Joanna and Mary were among your evangelists
    when they told their story to the men,
    who typically did not believe their "idle tale".
May we be diligent, faith-filled and bold as the women
    and like Peter who, though doubting,
    checked out this resurrection amazement.
Amen.

Luke 24.13-49

On that same day, O Risen Christ, you came near to fugitives
    escaping to melt into the countryside,
      on their way to a village with a reputation
      as a hideout for freedom fighters.
In their race to leave and lay low for a while,
    you entered their desperate conversation
      as they threw[24] words between themselves,
      maybe to blame for the failure, maybe to accuse the betrayers,
      maybe to concoct a cover story.
Having staked all on your messianic movement
    to rid their people of the yoke of oppression,
      they are amazed when you ask, "What things?"
As listening is at the heart of loving,
    you paid attention to their loss and bewilderment
      as wistfully, "They had hoped."[25]
By embracing their trauma and reigniting their hope,
    through the reframing of the story,
      pain and bitter disappointment leeched from their souls
      and the inevitability of your death became clear.
As their hearts burnt within them,
    they recognised you in the simple act of breaking bread.
Walk into our pain and bitter disappointment
    for those times we feel you do not deliver on our hopes.
Transform our wistfulness into reinvigorated hope.
Write into our hearts your death and resurrection mystery.
Amen.

---

[24] This is the literal meaning of the word used in the Greek.
[25] See v.21.

Luke 24.50-53

Returning out towards the house of welcome,[26]
    you completed your exodus of suffering
    through death and resurrection
    in the great prophetic tradition of Moses and Elijah.
Your leave-taking occurred in your ongoing spirit
    of generous goodness-giving for all the world,
    a spirit which endures for all time:
    joy-inducing; honour-generating.
O good news Christ,
    we are grateful for Dr Luke
    who ended his faithful witness as he started,
    with your people in the courts of the temple.
Place within our hearts the same passion and purpose
    that we may live as lovers of God
    and be dispensers of your generous goodness,
    serving as agents for healing
    in a world being made whole.
Amen.

---

[26] * *Bethany*, meaning "house of welcome" or "house of figs".

Prayer and the future of our species

To say, "The future of humanity will depend on our ability to pray," sounds rather pious, as if our survival is reliant upon the spirituality of a religious sub-culture that might be regarded as benign but slightly bizarre by many. Saying the daily office, having a quiet time, learning a discipline of silence or adopting a daily pattern of prayer are all good things, in theory at least. They are, though, only methods and habits, not the essence of prayer itself. It has to be noted, these are easier for some to embrace than others; to be honest, I often find them difficult.

Evolving our ability to pray runs in a parallel groove to our capacity to develop our consciousness. Such talk can appear a bit odd to many church folk and not seem very Godly. This, however, need not be the case.

Henri Nouwen once pointed out that when we use the word "prayer" it is usually because we feel our human limits have been reached. It indicates a state of need rather than a creative contact with the source of all life. Prayer needs to become something we live and inhabit, more than practices we verbalise.

We are not going to survive climate change, the depletion of natural resources and the pollution of the environment, nor truly make progress with women's rights, respect for minorities and fight injustice, unless we start to "see" from a different position, a different consciousness – we can call this prayer. Jesus taught his people to remain awake and alert.

Sadly, our sense of God can easily slip into images of an external operator or manager who intervenes occasionally in our reality. Or to switch analogies, God can be regarded as a sort of chess grandmaster who, from time to time, moves a piece on the board of our reality, but from a distance. This way of thinking affects how we pray.

Waking up and becoming more aware as individual human beings and as humanity as a whole is about seeing God in all things (the development of consciousness). This is more than finding God wherever we might look, but a recognition that God exists as part and parcel of the fabric of everything: in the energy of the smallest particle, in all forms of life and within the largest stars and black holes of the universe. As St Paul quoted, "In him, we live and move and have our being."[27] God is a part of the natural order even more than we are, and we are part of God more than we realise. Talking of our existence, the term "in Christ" appears in the New Testament seventy times or more.

When I worked as a jail chaplain, I used to explain to the prisoners our close connection of God as follows:

> Living and moving in God is a bit like being a fish.
> I am a fish.
> I am in God (the water).
> God is in me and I am mainly made up of God (water).
> I am not God (the water) though.

---

[27] Acts 17.28.

But I am more God than anything else.
God (the water) nurtures life while also being the
infrastructure of love in which I exist and operate.

Our survival as a species is not guaranteed as we now have the power to destroy ourselves. The evolution of our prayer and the development of our consciousness are crucial for our survival. True prayer changes us, rather than God.

You may wonder if I am pessimistic about the future. No, I am cautiously optimistic. There seems to be a greater interest in trying to look at reality from a different viewpoint (or you could say point of view). This may not always be prayer as we have traditionally understood it, but it is becoming apparent to me that our view of prayer is often corrupted by self-interest, the belief that God prioritises church people and our desire for personal comfort or power. The truth is we, as pray-ers, have a lot to learn.

So, we see through a glass darkly, as St Paul puts it, but will hopefully move to a place where we find prayer is less another activity we carry out and more an attitude we must live in and breathe from. This, I believe, has to be a part of our future, if we are to have one.

Thanks

My first thanks go to grandson Benjamin Andrew, born into our lives, bringing a wealth of gifts. He taught me how to rediscover the importance of the present moment as he lived in the fullness of each moment without worries for the future nor regrets about the past. He turned my ordered world upside as he adjusted to life outside his mother's womb and brought chaos to our home. From this disorientation he enabled me to look at afresh Luke's gospel.

There are those I travel with yet did not see during the pandemic season, nonetheless, I sensed they were very much my companions through emails exchanged, phone conversations enjoyed and books and articles shared. Our travelling days survived the storm and are hopefully enhanced by it.

No book gets this far without faithful friends who read through scripts to look for typos, crazy punctuations and nonsense sentences. So a big thank you to David Black, Joyce Williamson, Mike Owen and Dorothy Simpkin for taking the time.

I would not have made it this far through life so safely and healthily in body, mind and spirit for over four decades without Rosie; she is the greater half of the two of us (as many well know). I am truly thankful for her life.

Then there is the "Great Love", which at present is one of my favourite names for the one who we usually call God. (I agree with Eckhart Tolle who said, "The word 'God' has become empty of meaning through thousands of years of misuse.") So I say to this

Great Love, "Somehow I am in you and you are in me, far beyond my best understanding or most creative imagination. Despite my tenuous understanding, I hang on to you by your coattails in a ride that can sometimes be quite disturbing and upsetting, and at other times invigorating and wild; but like an old habit, I cannot give you up."

Also by Graham Turner

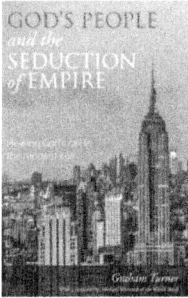

God's People
and the Seduction of Empire

"For those who still live in 'empire', a book like this is extremely helpful and important. In fact, without this wisdom and frame, the Bible has often ended up being a tool of oppression instead of a gift for liberation."

Richard Rohr, Author and founder
of the Centre for Action and Contemplation (New Mexico, USA)

"An accessible, radical and rare example of the aliveness and relevance of both the Old and New Testaments. Allow your faith to be energised and made passionate by reflecting on the insights that are brought to you in this book."

Ann Morisy, Community Theologian and Author

Available from www.sacristy.co.uk

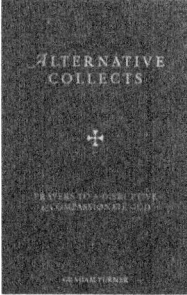

Alternative Collects:
*Prayers to a Disruptive
and Compassionate God*

"Graham Turner has written a new set of collects that follow in the wake of Cranmer. Turner fully understands and appreciates the force of the genre; his offer is a set of prayers that are fiercely timely, bold in their claims, and venturesome in their voicing. I cannot think of better access points to worship than those offered by Turner."

Walter Brueggemann, Columbia Theological Seminary

"Turner has written these prayers to introduce elements of risk, hope, challenge and creativity linked to the readings over the three-year lectionary cycle. Some are stunning prayers in the style of contemporary liturgical writing. They are less pithy than the psalm prayers, but with a similar bent towards social justice."

Dana Delap, Praxis News of Worship

Available from www.sacristy.co.uk

Other Media

www.facebook.com/OMG.TXTS

www.youtube.com/channel/UC0NI-XZnAJ2s7rXWkx_1Y-Q

https://twitter.com/GrahamCTuner

Notes

Printed in Great Britain
by Amazon